WATCHMAN NEE

Self-Knowledge and God's Light

Living Stream Ministry
Anaheim, CA • www.lsm.org

© 1992 Living Stream Ministry

All rights reserved. No part of this work may be reproduced or transmitted in any form or by any means—graphic, electronic, or mechanical, including photocopying, recording, or information storage and retrieval systems—without written permission from the publisher.

ISBN 978-1-57593-873-8

Living Stream Ministry
2431 W. La Palma Ave., Anaheim, CA 92801
P. O. Box 2121, Anaheim, CA 92814 USA

12 13 14 15 / 8 7 6 5 4 3 2

SELF-KNOWLEDGE AND GOD'S LIGHT

Today, I believe that God wants me to give a message on how to know ourselves. A Christian never progresses in spirituality if he does not know himself. And a Christian can never spiritually progress further than what he knows. Whatever light (not knowledge) he receives, he expresses life to that degree. No Christian can progress further than the light which God has given him. If a Christian does not know his faults or his real condition, he will not pursue after what is new or go on in the way ahead.

The most important thing in a Christian's life is to judge himself. He must consider his own flesh as not trustworthy and himself as absolutely useless. Only in this way will he utterly trust God. And only then can he walk according to the Holy Spirit and not according to the flesh. Without self-judgment, spiritual living is impossible. I have already spoken on this matter in another place; therefore, I shall not expand on it here. If one does not know himself, he will not judge himself and he will not have the spiritual blessings that come from self-judgment. God wants us to know how corrupt and how unable our flesh is to satisfy His demand. Because we do not know this, we fail to have the living which is purely in the Holy Spirit. Unconsciously we are filled with a heart of self-approval and self-confidence because of the shortage of self-knowledge. We consider ourselves trustworthy and fail to understand the meaning of the Lord's word, "Apart from Me you can do nothing" (John 15:5). Although the Holy Spirit is given to help our weaknesses, ignorance of our own weaknesses blinds us from looking for His help, and so we remain weak. If we do not know ourselves, we will not only be self-confident and self-approving, but we will also be full of self-content, thinking marvelously of ourselves and being full of a pride that is most displeasing to God. Because we do not know ourselves, our daily living will have many shortcomings. We will have no feeling about unfulfilled duties, unrighteousnesses toward others, instances of lack of love, and instances of being angry, anxious, and unmerciful.

Although the situation gets worse and worse, we feel at ease and content. Because we do not know ourselves, we do not know how great is our lack and how complete and precious is the salvation in Christ. As a result we miss so many spiritual blessings. Self-knowledge is the first condition toward betterment, because only those who know themselves desire for the better—yes, even God's best. Those who do not know themselves will not have a hungry and thirsty heart, and they will not have the filling of the Holy Spirit. Self-knowledge is absolutely indispensable to a Christian.

IS SELF-KNOWLEDGE DERIVED FROM SELF-EXAMINATION?

How do worldly people know their mistakes? They know by the method of introspection. They examine their own deeds and think back on their past. They "turn inward" to examine their motives and deeds. Introspection is commonly described as self-examination and evaluation. If worldly people do not examine themselves, they have no way of knowing themselves. I often hear many Christians say that they must examine themselves to see if they have committed any mistake. But let me tell you: *self-examination is not the duty of a Christian.* Self-examination is a big deception; many Christians are damaged by self-examination. We need to ask, (1) Does the Bible teach self-examination? (2) Can self-examination enable us to know ourselves? (3) Is self-examination profitable? From these we will prove that self-examination is really not the duty of a Christian.

1. Does the Bible Teach Self-examination?

Does the Bible command Christians to examine themselves? No! Griffith Thomas said that in the whole Bible there are only two places which mention self-examination, but both refer to something specific. Let us look at these two instances.

"But let a man prove himself, and in this way let him eat of the bread and drink of the cup" (1 Cor. 11:28). The proving in this verse is not an examination which Christians have in the pursuit of holiness; rather, it speaks of coming before the Lord to eat the bread and drink the cup. We should examine ourselves to see if we confess that the bread and the cup are the Lord's body and the Lord's blood. Eating the bread and drinking the cup is a testimony. Therefore, we must examine ourselves to see if we remember its spiritual significance; otherwise, it will become a ritual. Self-examination in this verse concerns whether or not we come to the Lord's table to remember the Lord. It does not ask us to turn inward to search for wrongs so that we can pursue after spiritual progress.

"Test yourselves whether you are in the faith; prove yourselves" (2 Cor. 13:5). This verse, even more than the first, does not tell us to examine our inward condition. This portion *indicates something specific.* At that time in Corinth, there were many who slandered Paul by saying that Paul was not an apostle. Therefore, Paul asked them, "Examine yourselves, whether you have faith or not. If you have faith, then that is the proof of my being an apostle. If God had not called me to be the apostle to the Gentiles, then how could you be saved? God called me to preach the gospel to you, Corinthians. Your salvation proves that I am a true apostle. If you have no faith, then I am a false apostle." The self-examination mentioned here is not a self-examination during our pursuit of holiness. Rather, it is a particular case of a particular condition existing in Corinth—a self-examination of whether or not there was faith.

In the Old Testament in the Chinese Bible, there is at least one more place which mentions examining oneself. "Examine your ways" (Hag. 1:5, 7). First, please take notice that it does not say that you must consider yourselves; rather, it says that you must examine your ways. This is outward. Second, the word *examine* in the original language means "to consider." It says that you must consider your outward behavior. It does not say that you should examine your inward condition.

When we read the context of the three portions mentioned above, we should realize that they are not talking about introspection. Rather, they talk about the examination of a *particular matter*. Therefore, we have the confidence to conclude that the Bible does not teach Christians to examine themselves.

2. Can Self-examination Enable Us to Know Ourselves?

Even if we examine ourselves, our experience tells us that we still cannot know ourselves. Let us see what the Bible says about us.

Jeremiah 17:9 says, "The heart is deceitful above all things / And it is incurable; / Who can know it?" Since our heart is deceitful, our self-examination will not be reliable. Because we are using a deceitful heart to examine ourselves, we cannot avoid being deceived by this deceitful heart. Perhaps you are wrong, but your heart may tell you that you are not wrong. Or perhaps you are not wrong, but because of some weaknesses, your heart may tell you that you are wrong. If the heart were proper, then it could be used as a standard; but, since the heart is deceitful, how can it be used as a standard? If you use an inaccurate standard to examine yourself, surely it will be hard for you not to be deceived.

A man was installing a chimney, and after he measured it with his ruler, he told the metal worker to make it ten feet long. When it was finished and delivered to him, no matter how he measured, it was one foot too long. He complained to the metal worker, and the metal worker measured it with his own ruler. It was exactly ten feet. However, the installer insisted that it was one foot too long. Eventually, the metal worker looked at the man's ruler and found that one-tenth of the man's ruler had been sawed off by his son who had played with it. Therefore, the chimney always measured one foot too long. If we would examine ourselves, we must first ask whether or not we are trustworthy. We have been corrupted and in the sight of God are very evil. How can we examine ourselves? Many think that self-examination is a virtue. But let me tell you: self-examination is a big mistake.

We have to know that the structure of our inward psychological parts is complex. Our desire, thought, feeling, and other manifestations of our heart are very complex. We cannot clearly analyze how they influence and interact one with the other. In such a complicated condition, even though we can examine ourselves, self-examination will never give us accurate self-knowledge. While you are examining your feelings, you do not know how your feelings are affected by and connected with all the other areas. Therefore, knowledge gained from your feeling is not trustworthy. Only a little influence can change your feeling completely. Many times concerning a certain matter we lose the proper view and do not have the accurate knowledge regarding our own intentions because there is a little hidden sin, wrong thought, or little prejudice inside us or because of our disposition by birth and innumerable other little causes. Any knowledge which we derive from ourselves is inaccurate because it is so complicated and untrustworthy.

We often come across a situation in which a person is very good on some point but does not know it; rather, he feels that he is weak on that point. On the other hand, he is weak on another point, yet he does not realize it but considers himself to be very good on that point. We often see this. This shows us that, even though man may examine himself, it is still impossible for him to know himself. Man cannot know himself through self-examination. I have a friend who talked very much about Christian love after he was saved. According to his view he considered himself to have much love, but in his home he was not at peace with his wife. Think about it! If one wishes to examine himself, is his self reliable? If his self is not trustworthy, then examining himself is useless.

Psalm 19:12 asks, "Who can discern his errors?" No one can know. We cannot know for sure our errors by ourselves.

3. Is Self-examination Profitable?

Not only is there no teaching in the Bible concerning self-examination and not only do our experiences tell us that we are incapable of examining ourselves, but also there is even great harm to our spiritual living if we examine ourselves. Self-examination will produce two kinds of results: either self-contentment or discouragement. When someone feels that he is quite good after self-examination, he becomes self-contented; when one feels that he is wrong after self-examination, he is discouraged. There is not a third result in addition to self-contentment and discouragement. God has taught me to know that no one can truly know himself through self-examination.

Hebrews 12:2 says: "Looking away unto Jesus...." In the original language between looking and Jesus there are some small words. We must translate it as "Looking away—unto Jesus." This means in order for you to look unto, you must first look away. You must first look away from what you should not be looking at; then you can look unto what you should. In Chinese we have an idiom "looking away completely" [Editor's Note: Wang Duan]. Therefore, I think this clause may be translated as "looking away completely—unto Jesus." Our spiritual living is based upon looking unto Jesus and not on turning back to ourselves. If we do not obey the command of the Bible to look unto Jesus but instead turn to look inside ourselves, we will suffer much spiritually. I have already said before that introspection—ourselves analyzing ourselves and our own feeling, intention, and thought—is most harmful. Griffith Thomas said, "There is now a common saying that if you look at yourself once, you must then look at Christ ten times. But I think this must be changed to look at Christ eleven times and do not look at yourself even once."

Two years ago I read a poem which was a fable. There was a centipede talking with a toad. The toad asked the centipede, "You have so many legs. How do you walk? Which leg do you move forward first when you walk?" The centipede then tried to determine which leg moved forward first when it walked. No matter how hard it tried, it could not set its feet right. Afterward it became tired and said, "I do not care. I'm leaving." When it started to go, it again thought of which leg to move first, and this inhibited it from taking any step. After a while sunshine came through the clouds. When the centipede saw the rays, it became very happy and ran toward the sun, forgetting all about the stepping order of so many legs. Thus, it was able to move once more. This fable is just a picture of our Christian living. The more we turn and look back, the more we cannot move and the more we retrogress. When we look at the light of the Lord, unconsciously we move forward.

Several years ago I read an article in an English magazine called *The Overcomers* which talked about very deep spiritual matters. The title of the article was "What Is Self?" The writer said, "Self is nothing other than one reflecting on oneself and one considering oneself." This sentence is truly deep and real. The time that our selves are active is when we turn and think of ourselves. We must remember that the soul is the feeling of the self. After the Welsh revival, there was a college professor who went to see the revivalist Mr. Roberts. The professor spent one day with him and talked with him about many questions. After he left, he wrote an article in the newspaper about his impression of Mr. Roberts. He said that Mr. Roberts was a man without any self-consciousness. Our defeat comes from too much consideration of ourselves; all we remember is our victory or our defeat. As a result, Christ cannot be completely manifested in us.

The way of our victory is not through a constant, unceasing analysis of ourselves. Rather, it is to look away unto Jesus. It is not the removal of evil thoughts, but the retention of good thoughts; it is not the eradication of something in ourselves, but yielding to the infilling of Christ in us to the extent that we completely forget about ourselves. Whenever we think back on ourselves, our steps are immediately halted. The Bible does not tell us to consider how we run. Rather, it tells us to run by looking away unto Jesus. If we turn to examine ourselves, we will see that we are in a fog; the more we examine, the more we become unclear. If we look away unto Jesus, we will naturally be able to run well.

When I was learning to ride a bicycle, many times I would ride it too close to the side of the wall and hit the wall. Every day I hurt my hand. Later I asked a schoolmate who could ride a bicycle to tell me my problem. When I rode on the bicycle, I fixed my eyes on the handlebars on the front of the bicycle, hoping that my hands might be steadier and the bicycle might not weave. But it did not work. The more I looked at the handlebars and tried to steady my hands, the more my hands trembled and the more the bicycle weaved. My schoolmate told me that I veered and hit the wall because I was looking at the handlebars and not the road. In order not to weave and hit the wall, *the eyes must keep looking at the road ahead.* Our living is the same way. Whenever we turn to look at ourselves, we will fail. We must look forward.

Many Christian failures are due to introspection and self-examination. When Christians turn to examine themselves, even if there is no other harm, they have lost at least one step. The Bible does not command Christians to examine themselves, because self-examination is not only unprofitable, but it hinders progress as well. Many Christians, after a day is over, review the things of the day and examine themselves. They are just fooling themselves. The apostle Paul did not care how others judged him. He did not even judge himself. He said, "Do not judge anything before the time, until the Lord comes, who will both bring to light the hidden things of darkness and make manifest the counsels of the hearts, and then there will be praise to each from God" (1 Cor. 4:5). Paul knew that only when the Lord shines His light can anyone know what is right and what is wrong. If a Christian repeatedly considers himself, he surely will fail. He will be proud and consider himself better than his companions when he thinks that he has no fault. He will be discouraged and see no way out when he thinks about his faults. If our self-knowledge comes from the shining of God, then the results will be different.

THE PROPER WAY

Do we mean to say that we can be careless about our daily life and need not ask whether our walk is right or wrong, or whether our intention is pure or impure? Our understanding is that the Bible does not teach us of self-examination, but we have not read that the Bible forbids us from knowing our self. Turning inward and thinking about oneself is harmful, but indulging oneself in looseness is even more harmful. God never allows us to be loose. Although God does not want us to examine ourselves, He wants us to know ourselves because the coming of the Holy Spirit causes man to reprove himself of his sin. According to the Bible, we should not pursue holiness through self-examination. This, however, does not mean that the Bible does not want us to pursue holiness. The Bible does not want us to know ourselves through self-examination, but this does not mean that the Bible does not want us to know ourselves. It is man's error to assume that self-examination and self-knowledge are inseparable. For this reason he thinks that refraining from examining oneself means that there is no need of knowing oneself. He does not realize that self-knowledge is still necessary, except that this self-knowledge must not come from self-examination. The goal remains the same. Only the way must be changed.

Since the Bible does not tell us to examine ourselves, what then is the way for us to know ourselves?

Let us read Psalm 26:2: "Examine me, O Jehovah, and try me; / Test my inward parts and my heart." And Psalm 139:23-24b says, "Search me, O God, and know my heart: / Try me, and know my thoughts: / And see if there be any wicked way in me." These two portions of the Scripture tell us the proper way to know ourselves. We do not need to strive in self-examination or ask ourselves how we feel about ourselves in order to know our inward parts and heart. Nor should we strive to know our heart and thoughts to see if there is any wicked way in us. Rather, the way is to ask God to search us and to try us. Only when God searches us and tries us can we have accurate knowledge concerning ourselves. Our self-knowledge does not depend on our self-examination. Rather, it depends on God's inspection.

These portions of the Scripture tell us that if we want the knowledge concerning ourselves, *we must ask God to tell us His knowledge about us*. This is the most accurate knowledge. God knows us more clearly and more accurately than we know ourselves. Everything is naked and open before Him. He sees and knows even the most hidden part of our heart, which we are not able to feel or analyze by ourselves. When we have His sight, then we will not be fooled and we will know our real condition.

Actually, only God's knowledge concerning us is correct. Do you know how God thinks about you? When you think that you are so good, does God also think the same thing? When you think that you are very bad, does God also think the same thing? When you feel that you are good, do not consider that you are good; when you feel that you are no good, do not consider that you are no good. This is not accurate. When God regards you as good, then you are good. And when God regards you as evil, then you are evil.

While God does not want us to examine ourselves, this does not mean that He does not want us to know ourselves or live carelessly. If we examine ourselves, we will still not be able to know ourselves. Maybe what He considers to be wrong, we think is good; what He considers as defilement, we think of merely as a little mistake. He wants us to have His same view. Therefore, He wants us to reject our untrustworthy feelings in deciding our condition and receive His thought and understand His judgment so that we may have an accurate assessment of ourselves.

GOD'S LIGHT AND SELF-KNOWLEDGE

How then can we know God's view concerning us? How can we enter into God's thought about us? Psalm 36:9 says, *"In Your light we see light."* In this verse there are two mentions of "light," and these two have different meanings. The first light is particular; it is "Your light"—the light of God. The second light is general; therefore, it says only "light" without using an adjective. The light of God is the knowledge of God; the sight of God is the view of God. To be in the light of God is to be exposed by God, to be told by God concerning what He knows. The second light means the real situation of a matter. Therefore, "in Your light we see light" means that when we receive the revelation of God, the shining of God's holy light, we are able to know the real situation of a certain matter. The matter will be clear as light in the eyes of our heart. In our own light we can never see light. Only in His light can we see light.

Ephesians 5:13 tells us clearly about the function of light: "But all things which are reproved are made *manifest* by the light; for everything that makes *manifest* is light." This tells us that the function of light is to manifest. The first light mentioned in Psalm 36:9 is objective, belonging to God. In this light we are exposed so that we see our real situation. This is the light which is seen in the light. We did not know our condition, but when the light of God shines, we see our condition. Many things which we have considered to be very good, when exposed one day under the light of God, we will realize are terrible. Perhaps we thought that we were better than everyone else, but when the light of God shines upon us, we see not only that sin is sin, but also many things which we considered to be good will be manifested to be sins. We should not make a self-examination and then report the results to the Lord; rather, we should be shined upon by the light and then confess before the Lord. Therefore, self-examination is not a virtue; it is a great mistake. It is not through self-examination, but rather through the light of God that we come to know ourselves. Only when we are in the light of God will we have the knowledge to know ourselves. As all the light of God concerning us becomes so bright, we will see what He sees in this light.

You do not have to ask when the light of God comes. Neither do you have to ask how I know that this is the light of God. There is no need for you to use a candle or a lantern to know the sun in the sky. As long as you can see yourself, you know that you are in the sunlight and that the sun has risen. Therefore, whenever the knowledge of yourself is so thorough and you see the true picture of yourself, utterly understanding the decadence of your own flesh, you will know that God has given you His light. Then you are in the light of God. If, however, your view about yourself is not as sober as the Bible's, if you do not feel that your flesh is as corrupted as the Bible says, and if you do not believe that you are as weak and despicable as the Bible says, then this proves that you have not received the light of God. You are not yet in the light of God. You do not have to ask where or what the light is. As long as you see the effect of light, you know what light is and where light is.

After Adam partook of the fruit of the tree of the knowledge of good and evil, the first thing he saw was his shame—nakedness. This was the *feeling of his own conscience*. He felt his own shame. But did he fear God? No, he still had his own method. He made an apron out of the leaves of a fig tree to cover his shame. When the voice of God came, asking him, "Where are you?" he hid among the trees in the garden to escape from the face of God. But he had no way. He could not depend on the apron he had made. He had to admit that he was naked. The result of self-examination is at best like Adam seeing his own shame. Not only did he not feel sorry for his sin; he tried to cover it. When God asked him the question, Adam really knew himself. God asked Adam, "Where are you?" Did God not know where Adam was? Certainly He knew. God asked so that Adam himself might know where he was. Those among us who have experience can testify that when we examine ourselves, even though we may see something wrong, we only cover it up by our own method. But whenever we are shined upon by God's light, there is no way to hide.

A certain believer asked a Jew whether or not he wanted to be saved, and he said no. The believer then compelled him to kneel down and pray that God would let him know himself. He realized how very filthy he was when the light of God shined. He saw his sins and wished that the floor would open up to swallow him. This shows us that a sinner needs the light of God to know that he is a sinner.

It is very hard for many sinners to confess that they are sinners before they are saved. Although many sinners are truly sinners in the view of others, they themselves do not feel like sinners. They will know how sinful and how wicked they are only when the light of God comes. The self-reproof produced by the light of God will cause them to feel that there is no hiding place. Many sinners know that they have sins. They feel this in their hearts and confess this with their mouths. To others, these people seem to have the wisdom of self-knowledge. But when the Holy Spirit sheds forth God's light, they realize that the sins which they have confessed are only superficial and that they do not hate sins the same way as God. After this enlightenment they will utterly feel that their sins are deplorable and that they need to seek deliverance. Let me add a word here: those of us who labor in the work of God must not convince others of their sins by our arguments; rather, we can only ask the Holy Spirit to do the work of reproving people of their sins. All kinds of self-examinations are equally shallow, inadequate, and erroneous. Only the light of God can cause man to see the picture of his true self as God sees him.

As Christians, day by day we know ourselves not through self-examination but through the light of God. When the light of God shines upon us, we will realize that we are corrupt to the uttermost. Perhaps we express much love to others. But when the light of God shines, we see that we have not loved others enough. We see that we are still short in many ways toward others. We gain many people and consider our work to be successful. But when the light of God shines, we realize that our works are nothing but the works of the flesh. They are vain and unprofitable. We begin to know that our works have not been done by God. Many times we think that we are doing the will of God wholeheartedly and that we are not seeking after anything for ourselves; but, when the light of God shines, we realize that we are not obeying the will of God. I once asked Miss Barber concerning her experience in obeying the will of God. She said, "Every time that God delays telling me His will, then I reckon that within me there is still a heart unwilling to obey the will of God. Within me there must still be an improper aim. I realized this from many experiences." When we seek the will of God and do not find an answer, we should ask God to search us to see if there is any unwillingness within us. When the light of God shines, we will see the inward situation. We think that we do not have any unwillingness within to obey God. But we are cheated by our own selves. When we wash our face, do we examine ourselves to see if there is white powder, black spots, or dirty mud on our faces, or do we look into the mirror to find out? If we want to know ourselves, we should not think about how we are, but ask for the shining of God's light. Only then will we know our condition. Many times we think that our intention is not wrong, but when God's light shines upon us, we realize how much selfishness, self provision, and even unrighteousness is within us. Without God's shining, we think our living is still acceptable. But when it is shined upon by God, we realize that we have failed. In the light of God, we can then see light.

The difference between a deep Christian and a shallow Christian hinges upon how much of the light of God they have received and whether it is permanent or temporary. Under the light of God, one sees black as black and white as white. The shallow Christian sees his shortages on a certain point only when he is exposed by God at a particular time. The deep Christian is constantly under God's shining, and he knows himself. Some of us here may have the following experience: we see a young Christian talking about his love for the Lord and how he has consecrated everything to the Lord. But we feel that he does not know what he is talking about. He still does not know how difficult it is to be consecrated to God and what the result of that consecration will be in the future. He only speaks according to his feeling at that moment.

This is like the Lord Jesus' response to James and John when they asked the Lord Jesus, "Grant to us to sit, one on Your right and one on Your left, in Your glory. But Jesus said to them, You do not know what you are asking. Are you able to drink the cup which I drink, or to be baptized with the baptism with which I am baptized? And they said to Him, We are able" (Mark 10:37-39). They did not know how deep and far-reaching were the things included in these two sentences. They hastily replied, "We are able." When we do not have the light of God, we are like these two disciples. We do not know how weak we are, and we do not know the extent of God's requirement upon us. We think we are able in everything. When the light of God shines, then we know that in many matters of spiritual truth, all we are saying are just words. We do not understand the meaning of them at all.

Not only will our goodness be manifested under God's light to not be good, but even what we normally consider as not good will be brought under God's light to a point where we further realize the extent of its not being good. Oftentimes we know very well that we are weak in certain points. We feel so. We tell others of the same, and we tell God this in our prayers. However, concerning our weakness, we do not have a deep enough feeling; we do not feel that it is so despicable. Moreover, although we know of this weakness, we still carelessly pass the days away. When the light of God comes, we will realize our weakness to the uttermost. Only then will we desperately feel the pain of this weakness and only then will we have a heart that deplores this weakness. Furthermore, we will feel that if we are not delivered from this, we cannot live on any longer. The difference in depth between the self-knowledge derived from our examination and the self-knowledge received from the light of God is too great to be measured. Therefore, friends, even if you know yourself, without the light of God you do not truly know yourself yet. Self-knowledge derived from examination merely demonstrates what you say about yourself. Self-knowledge received from the light of God demonstrates how God sees you. The judgment we have concerning ourselves can never be as accurate as the judgment of God concerning us.

Here we see the difference between the light of God and knowledge. Knowledge is what we know; it is understood in our mentality. The light of God is what God knows, and it is *revealed to us through His Spirit*. Many make a mistake in thinking that the light spoken of in the Bible means knowledge. For this reason we often hear people say that someone has much light, but his life is very poor. This cannot be so. Light is not knowledge. The Bible says that knowledge puffs up. But when the light of God shines into a man's heart, it does not puff him up. Rather, it causes him to reprove himself, repent of the past, hate the flesh, and beg in ashes for God to deliver him from his filthiness. It is possible for one to be full of biblical knowledge, yet at the same time, void of any of the light of God in his heart. If one has backslidden, he can still tell people about the Bible from his previous understanding, but he does not have the light of God. God's light is knowledge which is found in the power of the Holy Spirit, and knowledge is that light of God that is retained by man in his mentality. Knowledge has its place both in the Bible and in spiritual experiences, but knowledge apart from the power of the Holy Spirit is dead. Scofield said, "There is nothing more dangerous than when truth is divorced from power." Even though we may know much truth and receive much knowledge, we have no light and are not able to know our true condition or walk on the path ahead if these are not in the power of the Holy Spirit. If we have received light from God, we must then guard what we have received through the Holy Spirit who gave us the light, and we must make it the lasting light to our path, not letting it lose its power.

Oftentimes God gives us light and grants us true perception to a certain matter. During that time we seem to discern the deepest and the innermost part of the matter. It seems that everything is laid out before us and manifest in a naked way before our eyes. After a while, even though we still remember the experience and retain the knowledge, our feeling toward the matter seems to be not as deep, as if what we now see is not as clear as before. At this moment, the light of God is gone. What remains is nothing but knowledge. (Note: At the very least we must walk according to the knowledge we have. This does not mean, however, that it is enough just to have knowledge. We also need light.) Light can cause man to have the deepest feeling; knowledge cannot.

Therefore, if we want to walk in the path, the shining of God is indispensable. Our own feelings will either completely fool us or reduce the conviction of our sin. We will be following a blind guide if we are to pursue holiness through our feelings. There needs to be the light of God. Only then will the real condition of a matter be manifested. Light means how God sees our condition and what God says. When God says it is wrong, it is wrong. When God says it is one hundred percent wrong, it is one hundred percent wrong. Before the light comes, it is merely what you think and is not reliable. It is not what you say your life is, but what God says your life is.

When Miss Barber died, she left a Bible to me. Written in it were the words, "O God, grant me a thorough and unlimited revelation of myself." How deep is this! We often think that as long as we do not see anything wrong that this is good enough. Little do we realize that God has another kind of view regarding us. We will just be fooling ourselves if we do not receive the sight of God. We must have the boldness to be shined upon by God with His light so that He can reveal to us the real picture of ourselves. We have no way to know our own selves unless there is the shining of God. Our own evaluation of ourselves is not trustworthy.

WHERE DOES THIS LIGHT COME FROM?

First, Christ is our light. John 8:12 says, "Again therefore Jesus spoke to them, saying, I am the light of the world; he who follows Me shall by no means walk in darkness, but shall have the light of life." The Lord Jesus is light. When we draw near to the Lord, we shall see light. Often we think that this is quite good and that is not bad. But when we tell the Lord the facts of a situation, asking Him for enlightenment, we find to our surprise that everything is wrong. Day after day we think there is nothing wrong. But when we draw near to the Lord, everything is manifested to be wrong. One is our own standard, while the other is God's standard. When we draw near to the Lord, we will realize that our standard is not enough. If a Christian does not pray much for a revelation of his real condition, you can guarantee in nine cases out of ten that this Christian is in error. The more we draw near to the Lord, the more we will receive the light of God.

Second, the Word of God is our light. Psalm 119:105 says, "Thy word is a lamp unto my feet, and a light unto my path." Verse 130 says, "The entrance of thy words giveth light." These two verses may be very familiar to us, but if we read them carefully before God we will know how deep these verses are. Is the path in which you are walking justified by man or is it justified by God? The work of the flesh cannot escape the shining of the light of God. It is not what man says; rather, it is what the Word of God says. Day by day we should not follow our feelings in judging whether a matter is right or wrong. Rather, we must let the Word of God decide whether it is right or wrong. We ourselves should not judge. Rather, we should let the Word of God make the judgment. Put yourself in the Word of God, and let the Word of God judge, let the Word of God point out your real condition. For this reason, we must read the Bible more, and we must trust that the Holy Spirit would manifest the Word of God to us so that we may know ourselves.

Third, Christians are our light. Matthew 5:14 says, "You are the light of the world." We are very familiar with this verse. Normally we think that this verse speaks only of a Christian's good behavior. But actually there is a very deep meaning here. It says that a Christian is light. A Christian can illuminate the true condition of a man. Many Christians who are in the light of God, make other Christians afraid of seeing them because once they are seen, they will be condemned of their own sins. A weak Christian is not afraid of seeing another Christian who is in the same condition. But when you come close to a Christian who is in the light of God, you feel shameful. You were proud, but after being shined upon by him, you feel shameful. You were dishonest, but after being shined upon by him, you feel shameful. Brothers and sisters, we are the workers of God, serving God. If you do not have the light of God, you will not be able to work. People cannot be drawn closer to God by you if you do not have the light to illuminate them. If you draw near to God and are controlled constantly by the light of God, spontaneously you will illuminate the real condition of the people who are contacting you. If we want to obey the will of God and do the work of God, we need to be a light.

When you come close to Christians who are near to God, they make you feel God. They do not make you sense their tenderness and humility; rather, they make you feel God. When I began to work, I decided, at whatever cost, to obey the will of God. I thought I was obeying the will of God. However, whenever I went to see Miss Barber, after talking and reading a few verses from the Bible with her, I was aware that I was still lacking. Every time I saw her, I always felt something special—God was there. When you came close to her, you felt God. She had light. She was controlled by the light of God; therefore, when you came close to her, her light condemned your sin.

We must remember one thing. Whether by drawing near to Christ, by reading God's Word, or by being with other Christians, all the light we receive comes from the revelation of the Holy Spirit. It is the Holy Spirit who manifests the unapproachable light in which God dwells. It is He who manifests His glory, holiness, and righteousness. By this we see the absolute standard of God, so that we see ourselves, know our own real condition, and realize how we fall short of the standard of God.

THE POWER OF THIS LIGHT

The power of this light is the self-knowledge it renders to man. When a man gets into this light, it reveals to him his real condition. Many believers are very self-vindicating, self-satisfied, and full of self-pride. In this condition no human words, explanation, exhortation, warning, or reproof can make them see their own fallen state. Only when God gives grace and shines His light upon them through the Holy Spirit will this kind of person realize how corrupt, fallen, and hypocritical they are. When the light of God comes, everything changes color. In the light of God, everything shows its true color.

Actually, no man can be saved without being shined upon by God. No man can progress in the spiritual path and no man can have an effective work without being shined upon by God.

How can a sinner know that the Lord Jesus is the Savior? Surely not by argument. How can he know that he is a sinner? Surely not by reproof. No matter what method you use, whether arguing with the most logical words, debating with the most sufficient reason, or warning with the most stern words, none of these can make a sinner realize his own sins and see that Jesus is his Savior. I am not saying that all these methods are useless. They have their place. But they can only let people know mentally that they are sinners and that Jesus is the Savior. These methods can never cause them to *see*. Every sinner is blind, and this kind of blindness keeps him from seeing the true light of the gospel of God. The Holy Spirit opens the sinner's eyes through the light of God, enabling him to see the light of God. *Seeing* is a special blessing in the New Testament. God reveals His Son in me. This is an experience common to every saved sinner. It is most futile to get people to "receive Christianity," "believe in Jesus," and "become a Christian" by some beautiful thought, reason, warm feeling, emotion, music, tears, or argument. The light of God, the light that God emanates through the Holy Spirit, is the first indispensable element. The basic need is that a sinner must *see* his own condition and *see* the glory of Jesus. Getting him to shed tears, repent, be fervent, confess, and have good feelings are all futile. Only *seeing* in the Holy Spirit can cause a sinner to truly believe and receive the Lord Jesus as Savior. This is because you can never believe in what you have not seen, and you can never receive what you do not see. Because you have seen from within, you believe. Only this kind of faith is unmovable. Only this will withstand trials.

The progress of the Christian life does not depend upon many exhortations, warnings, and teachings. It is not a matter of telling a believer to be fervent, to do his duty, to read more of the Bible, or to pray more. All these are secondary; they are not primary. The primary element is to *see*. Therefore, when Paul wrote the letter to the Ephesians, though he knew that they were very good in the Lord and were not like the Corinthians who were so fallen morally, the first thing which he prayed for them was that God might *enlighten* the eyes of their hearts through the Holy Spirit. The progress of the Christian life is due to receiving the light of God, which opens a Christian's eyes and causes him to know the riches of the glory of God, and the greatness of the power of God that is given to him through the resurrection of Jesus Christ. If a Christian cannot see these things and does not know how rich these things are which he has received from God, then progress is an impossibility.

Anyone who is doing special work for God must be a person who has been shined upon by God. Only he who has been shined upon by God can judge his flesh. Only he who has judged his own flesh can be used by God. When the light of God comes, a believer is able to see how filthy he is because he has seen the holiness of God. He is able to know how unrighteous he is because he has seen the righteousness of God. He is able to know how corrupt he is because he has seen the glory of God. After a believer has known himself this way, he will be like one who is truly circumcised, not trusting in himself at all (not only not trusting, but deeply hating), but rather depending completely on the Spirit of God. Only this type of worker who is in the hands of God can be used by God. And only this type of worker can have the sight of God, seeing the plan of God and understanding the goal of God.

Because many people do not have the light of God, they consider themselves to be marvelous. Satan often cheats people by making them think that they have already obtained holiness and are sinless. Little do they realize that the reason they say this is because they do not have the light of God; hence, they do not know the corruption of the flesh. I am one who deeply believes in Christ being our life and that He can enable us to completely overcome sins. No Christian can excuse himself by saying that it is impossible for man to refrain from sin on this earth. But even if we are victorious, we cannot say that our flesh is not corrupted. There is a common error today: man either goes to one extreme or to the other. Some think that since they are corrupt, it is impossible for them not to sin. Others think that since they have received Christ to be their victory, sin is eradicated from within them, and therefore, they are no longer corrupt. Actually both of these are wrong. Truthfully, we are victorious in Christ, but we are corrupt in ourselves. A believer can have a life of complete victory over sin through Christ daily, and he can, at the same time, have the feeling every day that he is corrupt to the uttermost. The feeling of decadence and corruption cannot deter his victory because it is Christ overcoming in him and not himself. Likewise, his complete victory cannot remove from him the feeling of total corruption because the corruption of his flesh will not be changed in its nature by the deliverance of Christ.

Because so many have been deceived, thinking in their own small and dim light that they are so holy, sinless, and perfect in love, we need to see how many of the best and deepest saints in the Bible viewed themselves in the light of God.

Job

Job was a righteous man. This was God's remark about him. During the time of his suffering, his three friends thought that he had sinned and had offended God. But he himself denied this and used great efforts to argue with them to prove that he was clean and righteous. We all know that when God revealed Himself to him, the Bible recorded it and said: "I have heard of thee by the hearing of the ear; / but now mine eye seeth thee: / wherefore I abhor myself, and repent in dust and ashes" (Job 42:5-6). When the light of God came, he realized how despicable he was. The words of man could not make him reprove himself, but the light of God caused him to be humble.

Isaiah

Before God sent Isaiah, He first manifested His own glory to him. In this glory the prophet of God could not but cry: "Woe is me, for I am finished! / For I am a man of unclean lips, / And in the midst of a people of unclean lips I dwell: / Yet I have seen the King, Jehovah of hosts, with my eyes" (Isa. 6:5). Before he saw this vision, Isaiah's lips were unclean, and he was already dwelling in the midst of a people of unclean lips. But he did not feel it, and he probably thought that he could be a prophet serving God. When the bright light of God came, he was able to see the real condition of the people surrounding him. He was also able to see his own real condition, how unclean his mouth was and how unworthy he was to be a mouthpiece for God. So he cried, "Woe is me, for I am finished!" Truly, the holiness of God will bring out our "woe." After he knew himself in this way, the seraphim cleansed his mouth with live coal. Here we see a very good sequence: first uncleanness, then the light of God, then the self-knowledge of uncleanness, then the possibility of being cleansed, and finally the readiness to be sent.

Daniel

In the Bible there are two persons for whom there is no record of their sins. Daniel is one of them. From this, we know that before God he was pleasing to God. Yet the Bible tells us that when he saw the Lord and was shined upon by God, he said, "No strength was left in me, but my color turned deathly pale; and I retained no strength. Yet I heard the sound of His words; and when I heard the sound of His words, I fell into a deep sleep on my face, with my face to the ground" (Dan. 10:8-9). In the light of God, even the best saint cannot stand up. He had to bow to the ground.

Habakkuk

When Habakkuk was shined upon by God, he also had the same experience. He said, "I heard and my body trembled; / My lips quivered at the sound. / Rottenness entered my bones, / And I tremble in my place" (Hab. 3:16).

Peter

We know that Peter was a self-approving and self-trusting man. But when God shined a little bit of light through the Lord Jesus, giving Peter a glimpse of himself, he could not help but confess his own uncleanness. We know the story of how the disciples labored the whole night without catching anything. Then the Lord commanded them to cast the net in the deep water. They obeyed and caught many fishes, even filling up two boats. In this way the Lord manifested a ray of His glory and caused Peter to fall down at Jesus' knees, saying, "Depart from me, for I am a sinful man, Lord" (Luke 5:8).

Paul

Paul was the one who fought the good fight, finished his course, and kept the faith. When he was close to departing from this world, he told us, "I am the foremost" of sinners. What we want to note here is that the word "am" in the original language is in the present tense. This tells us how he considered himself at the time close to his death. He considered that the Lord Jesus came into the world to save sinners and that among the sinners he was the chief. He had nothing to boast about. He had no achievements; he had nothing special. He was like the other sinners, saved by the grace of Christ. Not only so, he considered himself to be worse than the others; therefore, he needed the grace of the Lord even more than they. Who has received more of the light of God than Paul? Because the light he received was more than that of the others, his self-knowledge was clearer than that of the others, and his self-judgment was more severe than that of the others. Only those without self-knowledge will consider themselves to be so holy, advanced, and special. The reason that they do not know themselves is because they have not received the light of God.

John

This disciple whom the Lord loved was

closer to the Lord than the others during the time when the Lord hid His glory in His flesh. Recall that he was the disciple who leaned on the Lord's breast. After the Lord's resurrection, he did good works for the Lord for several decades, and the Lord especially used him to write an epistle which specifically talks about fellowship and particularly about the love of God and the light of God. Humanly speaking then, if this disciple saw the light of God, he should not have been so fearful as many others. Yet recall that on the island of Patmos he described the Lord Jesus revealing His glory with the words, "His face shone as the sun shines in its power" (Rev. 1:16); and when he saw Him, he "fell at His feet as dead" (v. 17). There is no one who has seen the light of God who will not fall to the ground.

Not only do we see in the Scriptures how biblical men humbled themselves, confessed their sins, and obtained self-knowledge through seeing the light of God; even from church history, we see that many of the truly holy saints discovered their own weaknesses and corruption because of their closeness to God's light. Of the persons that we are about to cite, who can deny that they are the most outstanding people in the church? Yet how humble is the view they had of themselves. This is due to no other reason than that the closer we come to God, the more we discover our weaknesses. The more we receive the light of God, the more we realize our corruption. Those who are proud and self-approving are that way because they have not seen the light of God.

Martin Luther

When he was locked up in prison, he wrote a letter to one who was very powerful in the Roman church, saying, "Probably you may think that I am powerless now. The emperor can easily prohibit the petition of a pitiable monk such as I. However, you have to know that I will surely fulfill the responsibility which the love of Christ has placed upon me. I am not the least afraid of the power of Hades, let alone the Pope and his bishops." But when he saw himself in the light of God, this bravest of all reformers could not help but cry: "I am more afraid of my own heart than of the Pope and all his bishops. Within me there lies the biggest Pope—the self!"

John Knox

This Scot, for the sake of Christ, was a teacher, evangelist, prisoner, slave, wanderer, reformer, and statesman; at the same time, he was a saint of the rarest kind. In his very last prayer, he said: "This prayer is what I, John Knox, with my dying tongue and my whole mind, request of my God." In this prayer, there are the following sentences:

> O Lord, have mercy on me, do not judge my innumerable sins; amongst them, may you forgive especially those sins which the world cannot reprove. In my youth, my middle age, and until now, how much conflict have I passed through. I have discovered that within me there is nothing besides falsehood and corruption. O Lord, only You are the Lord who knows the secrets of man's heart. Please remember that of all the sins which I mentioned, not one of them is pleasing to me. I often grieve over them: they are deeply hated by my inner man.

Now I weep sorrowfully for my
corruption. I can only rest simply
in Your mercy.

This is the prayer of a man who has been shined upon by God.

John Bunyan

John Bunyan was put in prison for thirteen years because he wanted to preach the gospel. In prison he wrote the well-known book, *Pilgrim's Progress*. Except for the Bible, *Pilgrim's Progress* may have the most translations in the world. Spurgeon said of him, "In my view, the style of John Bunyan most resembles the style of the Lord Jesus; no man can come close to him." But when Bunyan wrote about himself, he said,

> After my previous repentance,
> there is again one thing which
> makes me sad; that is, if I most
> severely examine the best thing
> I am now doing, in it I discover
> sins, new sins mingled in the best
> thing I do. Therefore now, I can-
> not help but conclude that no
> matter how proud of myself and
> how idealistic I was concerning

> myself and my work, and even if
> my former living were without
> blemish, yet the sins that I com-
> mit in a day are enough to send
> me to hell.

In such a deep feeling of sins, he cried out: "Unless He is such a great Savior, He surely cannot save such a great sinner as I."

George Whitefield

This extraordinary evangelist, who is as famous as John Wesley, when he was dying, said,

> Oh, may I be able to lie down
> and die in the labor of my Lord,
> for I consider it worthwhile to
> die for this. If I have a thousand
> bodies, every one of these bodies
> will be a wandering evangelist
> for Jesus.

The last time he retired to rest, holding a candle, there was a big flock of people surrounding his doorway, asking him to preach to them once more. He knew that he was dying that day, yet he preached to them until the candle burned out, and then he went upstairs to die. When this man talked about himself, he said,

In the fulfilling of all our responsibilities there is always corruption mixed within it; therefore, after our repentance, if Jesus Christ would only receive us according to our deeds; then our deeds would surely condemn us because we cannot offer a prayer which is as perfect as that required by the moral law of God. I do not know how you might think; but I can say that I cannot pray, I can only sin; I cannot preach to you or to others, I can only sin; I can only say this: even my repentance needs repenting again; even my tears need to be washed in the precious blood of my Redeemer. The best deeds we have are but sins with spectacles.

Augustus Toplady

This very godly person, when he counted his sins, considered that every second he committed at least one sin. That is to say that in ten years, there were more than three hundred million sins. Therefore, he wrote that glorious hymn which caused millions of people, who were tired and oppressed by sin, to find rest—"Rock of Ages, cleft for me, / Let me hide myself in Thee"! He wrote,

> Oh, is there one as pitiable as I in this world! Besides weakness and sin I have nothing. In my flesh there is no good thing, and how surprising that I could be tempted to view myself so high. The best work I have done in my life only qualifies me to be condemned.

But when he was dying of tuberculosis in London, he leaned his sinful head on the breast of the Savior and said, "I am the happiest man in this world."

Jonathan Edwards

He was a very spiritual man who was greatly used by the Lord. Whenever he preached, countless people wept for their sins, as if pricked in their hearts, and asked forgiveness of the Savior. He was a most honest man, so he wrote the following very humbly:

I often feel most deeply how I myself am filled with sins and filth; very often because this feeling is too strong, I cannot help but cry aloud. Sometimes I cry for so long, so that I have no alternative but to lock myself up often. Now I feel very deeply the wickedness of myself and the corruption of my heart, even more severely than before my conversion. Speaking of myself, I have long felt that my wickedness is completely incurable; it fills my thoughts and imaginations. Yet at the same time I feel that my sensitivity toward sins is too little and too slight; I am surprised that I actually cannot have more sensitivity toward sins. What I most hope for now is to be able to have a contrite heart and to most humbly prostrate myself before God.

David Brainerd

Oh that the things that were

> seen and heard in this extraordinary person, his holiness, heavenliness, labor, and self-denial in life, his so remarkably devoting himself and his all, in heart and practice, to the glory of God, and the wonderful frame of mind manifested, in so steadfast a manner, under the expectation of death, and the pains and agonies that brought it on, may excite in us all a due sense of the greatness of the work we have to do in the world, the excellency and amiableness of thorough religion in experience and practice, and the blessedness of the end of such.

These are the words of Jonathan Edwards at the burial of David Brainerd, who became his son through the gospel. When Brainerd was twenty-five years old, he labored among the poor Indians in the heart of the forest in America. He labored, he suffered, he prayed, he fasted until the Spirit of God was poured upon them, so that many repented, turned to the Lord, and lived for the Lord. Five years later, he rested.

Yet concerning himself, he sighed this way, "Oh, the filth within me! Oh, my shame and sins before God! Oh, the pride, selfishness, hypocrisy, ignorance, bitterness, party zeal, and the lack of love, candor, gentleness, and peace that have attended my attempts to promote the interests of religion!"

Hudson Taylor

The head of the China Inland Mission in Canada, Mr. Frost, was a co-worker of Hudson Taylor for decades. He said that he prayed with Hudson Taylor hundreds or even thousands of times, yet not once did he hear Mr. Taylor pray without confessing his sins.

These are men who drew close to God more than others; yet surprisingly, they had these kinds of feelings about themselves. Let me ask a question. Can ordinary believers, who are not as close to God as these and do not sense their own corruption, be more advanced than these men? Everyone would answer, No. If they do not sense their shortcomings, it does not mean that they are good. On the contrary, this only shows that they lack the enlightenment of self-knowledge. The reason that these men could sense their own unworthiness was because they were especially close to God. They received more of the light of God than others. They knew the absolute measure of the holiness of God. Therefore, they felt their own shortcomings more than the others. First John tells us, "But if we walk in the light…the blood of Jesus His Son cleanses us from every sin" (1:7). Because we are in the light, sins are manifested and the blood of Jesus becomes necessary. Then it continues: "If we say that we do not have sin, we are deceiving ourselves, and the truth is not in us" (v. 8). Those who say that they have no sin are self-deceivers. The reason that they can deceive themselves is because truth—the truth that comes from the light of God—is not in their heart. Only those without the enlightening of God will consider themselves to be good, holy, perfect, and sinless. If we draw close to God as these men did, then we will surely also sense our own filthiness. The more we draw close to God, the higher our measure of holiness and the more we will know what is filthy, corrupt, and unrighteous.

The depth of our feeling toward sin varies with the amount of the light of God that we have received. We did not consider many things to be sin at the start of our Christian living. When we progressed in grace, we understood those things were also sins. Many things which we considered right last year, we discovered were wrong this year because we have received more of the light of God. Perhaps many things which you now consider as acceptable will appear wrong when more of God and His intention is unfolded to you. There is not one Christian in the world who is completely without fault. We have to be careful and not be deceived by the flesh in thinking that we have now attained "sinless perfection."

THE FUTURE JUDGMENT

We know that we Christians have to stand before the judgment seat of Christ in the future and be judged. This judgment does not decide whether or not we shall be saved for eternity. It decides whether or not we can enter into the kingdom and what will be our place in the kingdom. This judgment by the Lord concerns our daily living and work which we have after we are saved. Whether or not we shall receive praise from God in the future depends on whether or not we have obeyed the will of God today. Aside from His will, God is pleased with nothing else. Whether or not we receive a reward is a small matter, but whether or not the Lord's heart is pleased and satisfied is a big question. I believe that every saved person has a common desire to please the Lord, though the degree of the earnestness of this desire might differ.

Among many believers who want to "gain Christ," some often carelessly say that this is the will of God or that is the will of God; or I feel that this is God's leading or that is God's leading. Beloved, do you know that these things have to go through the judgment of God in the future? It is not what we say that counts, nor what we feel that counts. It is not what we consider or believe that counts; rather, it is a matter of whether or not our work is really out of the will of God. First Corinthians 3 tells us the way we will be judged in the future: "The work of each will become manifest; for the day will declare it, because it is revealed by fire, and the fire itself will prove each one's work, of what sort it is" (v. 13). What is this fire? We know the function of fire. Sometimes it is used to burn, but often it is used to illuminate. For the work of wood, hay, and stubble, the fire is for burning. But for the work of gold, silver, and precious stones, the fire is for illuminating. If we put this verse together with Revelation 1:14, which describes how the eyes of the Lord of judgment are like a flame of fire, we can understand more the meaning of this fire. When we are judged in the future, the Lord will use His fire to test our work, to manifest our work. This fire is His eyes which are like flaming fire. This means that the Lord will judge through His light and according to His view all the work we have done after we were saved. His light will reveal what is according to His will and what is not.

Let us be assured that before God there is only one right or wrong, and there is only one standard of right and wrong. This standard is absolute, perfect, unchangeable, and unmovable. We will be judged in the future according to this standard. No matter what we say, how we feel, what we believe, or what we think, if our walk is not really of the will of God today, then in that day we will surely suffer loss. In the light of God, not only will it be impossible for anything to be hidden, but it will also be impossible for anything to be wrong. Today if we do not have the light of God to reveal our real condition and to tell us whether or not a matter fits His will, then in that day when God will judge through His light and according to His will, we will surely be unable to stand. If we have the shining of God in every aspect and we know His will (whether it is towards ourselves, towards others, or towards a certain thing) while we live on this earth, then in that day our work will surely receive a reward. Let us be assured that the light of God we receive for work today will be the light which God will use to judge us in the future. Therefore, if we want to know whether or not our work can stand in the light of God in that day, then we must ask whether or not our work today is done according to the light of God. Let me tell you, the light of God never changes. Whatever the light of God condemns and considers as contrary to His will today, the light of God will surely condemn and consider contrary to His will in the future. Whatever the light of God approves and considers in agreement with His will today, the light of God will also approve and consider in agreement with His will in the future. We should never risk the danger of walking contrary to the light of God, neglecting the will of God, and ignoring the view of God, while wishing to receive a reward at the day of the revelation of God's light.

What we daily live by now is the light of God. When we say that we are now walking according to the light of God, we mean that we are walking according to the judgment of God and that we have a clear vision of how God will judge our daily walk in the future. Since we are so clear concerning the situation at the coming judgment seat, we should be compelled before God, through this knowledge, to do that which will receive praise from Him, rather than that which will be condemned by Him at that day. The light of God is the light before the judgment seat. If we know ourselves through the light of God and walk according to the knowledge of His will through the light of God, then we know ourselves through the light before the judgment seat and walk according to the knowledge of His will through the light before the judgment seat. We ought to thank and praise God because we do not have to wait until that day to see the light of God and know how He will judge us. Today we already have the possibility of seeing the light. Today we already may know what He will condemn in the future and what He will approve in the future. The Holy Spirit comes to dwell in our heart to reveal the light of God; therefore, our responsibility is inexcusable.

Paul considered the future judgment of God to be according to the light of God. He told us that the things done according to our feelings were worthless. Therefore he said: "For I am conscious of nothing against myself; but I am not justified in this, but He who examines me is the Lord. So then do not judge anything before the time, until the Lord comes, who will both bring to light the hidden things of darkness and make manifest the counsels of the hearts, and then there will be praise to each from God" (1 Cor. 4:4-5). This portion of the Bible cannot be more clear. Brothers, if the feeling of a man such as Paul was unreliable, who knew of no wrong in himself and still did not regard himself as justified, how about you and me? He said that unless God shines upon us with light in that day, there are many hidden things and thoughts which can influence our actions and cause us to walk our own ways. In that day when

God shines on us, then we will know how much we were influenced by that which was hidden. Therefore, he told us in the previous verses that besides being faithful, he had nothing. If we set ourselves to be faithful, willing to pay any price to obey the will of God, then God will surely tell us His will so that we will know what to do. The Lord Jesus said, "If anyone resolves to do His will, he will know" (John 7:17).

Therefore, brothers, if we seek the light of God now on earth, when we see this light manifested in the future, we will not be condemned, but rather we will receive a reward of full satisfaction.

A PRAYER

We know how important it is to obey the will of God. But if we want to know His will, we must have a heart before God that is willing to do His will. Our heart must be weaned from everything. We must have only one desire before God, that is, to know the desire of His heart. No matter what God reveals, we are willing to receive it. In this kind of condition and with this kind of tender and obedient heart, God will surely tell us His will. "The intimate counsel of Jehovah belongs to those who fear him; /

And His covenant He will make known to them" (Psa. 25:14).

Many times we do not know our heart. We do not know how treacherous, how crooked, and how rebellious our heart is. We think that we are willing to obey, that we really desire the will of God, but we do not realize that in the deepest part of our heart there are hidden motives and self-will. Therefore, we must cry as David cried before God, "Examine me, O Jehovah, and try me; / Test my inward parts and my heart" (Psa. 26:2). "Search me, O God, and know my heart: / try me, and know my thoughts: / and see if there be any wicked way in me, / and lead me in the way everlasting" (Psa. 139:23-24). Only when God searches us and knows our heart will we know our heart. Only when God tries us and knows our thoughts will we know our thoughts. When we pass through this kind of searching and trying by God, we will be able to see if there is any wicked way in us—any wicked intentions, so that we may deal with them and be led of God to walk the way of eternal life. Many believers want to understand the will of God. They ask God to tell them His will. Yet they have not received it. There is no reason other than they have wicked ways in their hearts, which makes it impossible for God to lead them. They do not know themselves. They do not know how much inclination, how much opinion, how much fear, and how much lust are in their own hearts. These make it impossible for God to reveal His will. If before God they would ask Him to shine upon them, grant them self-knowledge, and then remove their obstacles, God would surely lead them. Although self-knowledge cannot immediately make known the will of God, self-knowledge can make known what is hidden in us that frustrates the understanding of God's will. Therefore, self-knowledge is indispensable in understanding the will of God. Without the light of God, who can know himself? Therefore, is it not the time for us now to pray the same way as David prayed?